a quivering jelly. You'll also find lots of advice to help you bust those bullying blues.

So why suffer bullying in silence? Let's make it extinct together...after all, the pun is mightier than the sword!

By the same author

The Little Book of Cool at School
The Little Book of Cool at Christmas
The Little Book of Summer Cool

John Byrne

RED FOX

The author and publishers of this book are grateful to KIDSCAPE, for allowing them to use information found in their publications *You Can Beat Bullying!* and *Stop Bullying!*

A Red Fox Book

Published by Random House Children's Books
20 Vauxhall Bridge Road, London SW1V 2SA

A division of The Random House Group Ltd
London Melbourne Sydney Auckland
Johannesburg and agencies throughout the world

Printed and bound in Great Britain by
Cox & Wyman Ltd, Reading, Berkshire

The RANDOM HOUSE Group Limited Reg. No. 954009

Papers used by The Random House Group Ltd are natural, recyclable products made from wood grown in sustainable forests. The manufacturing processes conform to the environmental regulations of the country of origin.

www.randomhouse.co.uk.

ISBN 0 09 960981 9

GET BUSTING!

If School Bully's nose could talk what would it say?
'Stop picking on me!'

What's the difference between a wild boar and School Bully?
One is a big, smelly, bad-tempered beast and the other is an animal.

What did the pig say when it saw School Bully?
'Snap!'

Why are School Bullies like bananas?
Because they are yellow and hang around in bunches.

What sound do you get if you cross School Bully with a watch?
Thick tock.

Why did School Bully have a sausage on his forehead?
Because he's a head banger.

School Bully is very good at animal impressions. He doesn't do the sounds...
just the smells.

Teacher: 'Put that mirror away – you've been looking at yourself all through the lesson!'
School Bully: 'But Sir – you told me I'd have to watch my behaviour!'

Class 3B were on a cross-country run and Nadia was in the lead. Suddenly School Bully thundered up behind her and pushed her roughly out of the way.

'Pig!' shouted Nadia.

'I'll get you for that!'

School Bully shouted back – and then tripped over a pig in the middle of the road.

School Bully: 'Doctor, Doctor, I've got a terrible stomach ache. There must have been something wrong with the bananas I stole from Mary Smith's lunchbox!'

Doctor: 'Well, what did they look like when you peeled them?'
School Bully: 'You mean you're supposed to peel them?'

What's got long ears, a cotton tail and no friends?
Bugs Bully.

I have a soft spot for School Bully. I've covered up the sign saying: 'Danger: Quicksand'.

Why did School Bully drop his playing cards in the mud?
So he could get up to his usual dirty tricks.

The last time I saw a face like School Bully's, it was a bottom!

School Bully: 'You look really ugly.'
Ahmed: 'And you look perfectly normal....
Normal for a gorilla, that is!'

School Bully is a very responsible pupil. If there's any trouble at school he's the one responsible.

'School Bully thinks he's really hard...'
'He is now – we've just poured cement over him.'

School Bully: ' I want to phone a friend – give me ten pence or else!'
Jason: 'Here's twenty pence – phone all your friends!'

I SEE SCHOOL BULLY'S GETTING A TASTE OF HIS OWN MEDICINE!

BULLY CURE

First School Bully: 'I'm going to bash that Natalie! She called me thick, ugly and smelly!'
Second School Bully: 'Don't pay any attention to her – she's only repeating what everyone else says!'

School Bully:
'You smell funny!'
Claudette: 'It's soap – I knew you wouldn't recognise it!'

WHAT'S THE DIFFERENCE BETWEEN SCHOOL BULLY AND A RUBBER DUCK?

NOTHING... THEY'RE BOTH QUACKERS!

ANNUAL BATH TODAY

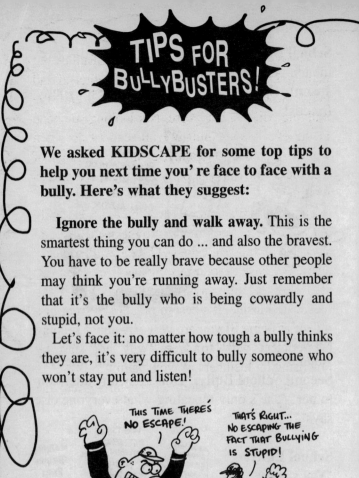

TIPS FOR BULLYBUSTERS!

We asked **KIDSCAPE** for some top tips to help you next time you're face to face with a bully. Here's what they suggest:

Ignore the bully and walk away. This is the smartest thing you can do ... and also the bravest. You have to be really brave because other people may think you're running away. Just remember that it's the bully who is being cowardly and stupid, not you.

Let's face it: no matter how tough a bully thinks they are, it's very difficult to bully someone who won't stay put and listen!

Always look the bully in the eye. Bullies get their kicks out of making you feel frightened and helpless. Give them what they want and the bullying will just get worse. Not looking someone in the eye is something we all tend to do when we're frightened of them. But it's a real sign of weakness, and tells the bully that their evil plan is working.

That's why it's better to do something the bully *doesn't* expect. Look them straight in the eye and say, 'No – this isn't funny!' then walk quickly away. You have to sound strong and firm when you say, 'No!' and this can be difficult especially if you feel scared inside. It's best to practise in front of a mirror at home. If you are very shy about keeping eye contact with strangers, why not start by practising on members of your family?

You'll find lots more advice throughout the following pages...

Why does Red Fox never bully?
Because bullies are usually chicken.

What did Father Christmas do to the bully
reindeer?
He gave him the sack.

'If I catch you bullying again, I'm going to tell your parents,' said the teacher.
'Oh Sir, you didn't ought to do that!' said School Bully.
'Tsk, tsk. Where's your grammar?'
'She's busy causing trouble down at the Old Folk's Club.'

What do you call School Bully in a rocket?
A waste of space.

Why won't anyone play with School Bully?
Because he's lost his marbles.

Did you hear about the bully who fell through the floor of the Assembly Hall?
It was just a stage he was going through.

UH OH! LOOKS LIKE SCHOOL BULLY'S GOT THE WIND UP AGAIN...

BURP!

BEANS

School Bully: 'Doctor, Doctor, I keep thinking I'm an elastic band.'
Doctor: 'That's no reason to keep snapping at people.'

'Doctor, Doctor, since I've become School Bully, nobody wants to talk to me.'
'Next.'

George: 'Do you know the difference between a clock and a pupil?'
School Bully: 'Of course I do.'
George: 'Well, stop winding me up then!'

'Doctor, Doctor, I've been a bully for as long as I can remember.'
'Really? I wonder what started it?'
'Started what?'

Ramon: 'Don't you think you need glasses?'
School Bully: 'What's it to you?'
Ramon: 'Nothing – but you've just spent five minutes telling that dustbin that you're going to thump it!'

School Bully: 'Why do you think I'd make a good baker?'
Careers Teacher: 'Because you seem to spend most of your time loafing around!'

Anita: 'You remind me of a peach...'
School Bully: 'You mean I'm sweet with very soft skin?'
Anita: 'No. You've got a heart of stone!'

School Bully: 'Doctor, Doctor, everyone says I've got a big mouth. What can you give me to help?'
Doctor: 'A bigger toothbrush?'

Knock knock.
Who's there?
Felix.
Felix who?
Felix-tremely silly since I started bullying people.

WHAT DID SCHOOL BULLY SAY AFTER HE TRIED TO TEASE THE WITCH'S CAT?

HE SAID "RIBIT, RIBIT RIBIT"!

School Bully: 'If I hear any of you lot talking about me, I'll thump you!'
Kids: 'But you can't do anything to us for just thinking, can you?'
School Bully: 'Er, no...'
Kids: 'Good – because we all think you're a plonker!'

We were tucking into our lunch when School Bully arrived and demanded that we each give him a roll.
So we pushed him down a hill.

School Bully: 'Give me all your money!'
Mary: 'No way – that's my money for the school trip.'
School Bully: 'So what? I fancy going somewhere I haven't been before...'
Mary: 'Why not try the bathroom?'

Why did the cow never get picked on by bullies?
She made sure never to stray too far from the udders.

Why are bullies like toenails?
Because the sooner they are cut down to size the better.

School Bully's not just a good Boxer ... he looks like other dogs too!

Why did School Bully lock himself in the fridge?
It was the only way he could look cool.

What do you say to a Bully Kangaroo?
'Hop it!'

Why did School Bully throw away his compass?
Everyone kept telling him to get lost.

Knock knock.
Who's there?
Justine.
Justine who?
Justine-side every school bully, you'll find a
great big coward.

SCHOOL BULLY FELL IN THE CEMENT...

WELL, SHE ALWAYS WAS SET IN HER WAYS!

School Bully burst into the classroom holding a
sheet of paper.
'Right! Which one of you stuck up this picture
of me with BULLIES ARE STUPID on it?'
'We all did!' said the class and surrounded him.
'Er – I just wanted to congratulate you on
having such neat writing...'

What do you get if you cross School Bully with
the school cat?
A *Sourpuss.*

WELCOME SCHOOL BULLY— YOU CAN START BY EXERCISING YOUR MOUTH LESS AND YOUR BRAIN A BIT MORE!

What do you call School Bully when he's got his finger in his ear?
A space probe.

What do you call School Bully when he's got two fingers in his ears?
Anything you like he can't hear you.

What does School Bully call you when you're with ten of your friends?
Sir.

School Bully: 'This school isn't big enough for both of us!'
Shanice: 'Good luck with your diet, then!'

What do you get if you cross School Bully with a yellow pudding?
Cowardy custard.

TIPS FOR BULLYBUSTERS!

More suggestions from KIDSCAPE:

Never show that you are upset. No matter what horrible things the bully says to you don't let them see that you are upset. This is just what they are after. If you can keep calm and ignore them, bullies often get bored and give up.

You can also try to make a joke of the whole thing and think of clever answers to their taunts. (This isn't as hard as it sounds – it doesn't take much to be smarter than a bully!) You might even be able to use some of the jokes and snappy answers in the *Bullybusters Joke Book*. Again, practising in front of a mirror will help you speak firmly. (Just remember that the idea *isn't* to get into a shouting match – as soon as you zap them with your snappy answer, start walking away as the bully's tiny brain is straining to think of a reply!)

Don't get into a fight. Since most bullies only pick on people weaker than they are the chances are you will get hurt. Sometimes it can be very tempting to fight. Friends, parents and other adults may even *encourage* you to fight back. Big mistake. Most of the time meeting violence with violence just makes things even worse. Besides, you might even end up getting blamed for starting the fight!

The same applies when it comes to money or possessions. Sometimes the smartest thing to do is to hand them over. Property can be replaced – you can't.

MIRROR, MIRROR ON THE WALL...

...LET'S MAKE THOSE BULLIES FEEL REALLY SMALL!

VICTIM

BULLY BUSTER!

What do you get if you cross School Bully with the yellow brick road?
The Wizard of Yob.

What do you get if you cross School Bully with an owl?
Something that no one likes but it doesn't give a hoot.

What's the difference between School Bully and a vampire?
Nothing – they're both a pain in the neck.

School Bully turned up at school one morning with a huge pit bull terrier.
'You can't bring that savage ugly creature into class,' said the Headmaster.
'It's not my fault,' said the pit bull terrier. 'He followed me here.'

Why is School Bully like a calendar?
Because his days are numbered.

School Bully took his seat in the classroom. But the teacher made him put it back.

Why did the headmaster punish School Bully for throwing jelly and sponge around the canteen?
Because he didn't like being trifled with.

School Bully was working on the school magazine
... well, actually he was annoying everyone else as
usual. Until little Urmi jumped on a chair, rolled up
a copy of last term's issue and walloped him on the
head.
'Hey! You can't do that!' said School Bully.
'Yes I can,' said Urmi. 'After all, I *am* the 'ed-itor!'

School Bully: 'I'm a big noise around here!'
Nigel: 'Well tell your mum to stop giving you
baked beans for breakfast!'

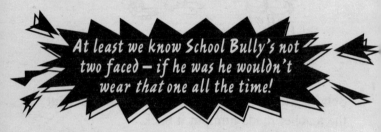

At least we know School Bully's not
two faced – if he was he wouldn't
wear that one all the time!

What did School Bully say when she got ten
valentine cards?
'Where are the other twenty I posted?'

When School Bully was born it wasn't a stork
that delivered him – it was a vulture.

'You've been misbehaving all year,' said School
Bully's mum. 'But don't worry. You're still going
to get something on your birthday.'
'Great,' said School Bully. 'What am I getting?'
'Older.'

School Bully's mum was so sick of him looking scruffy that she bought him a pocket comb. But he never uses it. He says he doesn't need to comb his pockets.

Why do all the school-kids fight over School Bully's friendship?
Nobody wants to be the one stuck with it.

School Bully: 'Cock a Doodle Doo!'
Teacher: 'I've warned you before about using fowl language.'

The art teacher has banned School Bully from the darkroom. Every time he's allowed in there, trouble develops.

'I'm going to have to stop pulling ugly faces.'
'Why is that?'
'Because School Bully's going to thump me if I pull his anymore.'

'I think I've worked out what's wrong with School Bully. He's not bad, he's just been made upside down.'
'How do you mean upside down?'
'Haven't you noticed? His nose runs and his feet smell.'

There are really only two things wrong with School Bully. Everything he says and everything he does.

School Bully's improving a bit. He always used to steal people's watches in the playground and then eat them, but now he's stopped. He said it was much too time consuming.

WHAT DO YOU CALL A BIG BULLY WHO RUNS AWAY AS SOON AS WE STAND UP TO HIM?

A YELLOW-PHANT!

'You can go, School Bully,' said the Headmaster sadly. 'But I'm still not convinced that you haven't been stealing things from the school canteen.'
'Of course I haven't, Sir,' said School Bully.
'Does this mean I can keep the sausages?'

Why is School Bully like a river every morning?
Because he doesn't want to leave his bed.

Why did School Bully get into trouble when he tried to step on an ant.
Because it was an eleph-ant.

'Hey School Bully, does *everyone* in your family wake up grumpy in the morning?'
'They don't have to – I've got my own alarm clock.'

School Bully was a big hit in the school play. Mostly he got hit by eggs and rotten tomatoes.

What did the head of the witch high school do to School Bully?
She gave her extra spelling lessons.

School Bully's report card says that he's a thug, a yob and very bad-mannered.
All his teachers are really pleased with how much he's improved since last term.

Where does School Bully keep souvenirs of all his fights?
In his scrap book.

Why did School Bully squirt lemon juice into his eye.
It was the only way to make himself smart.

School Bully is a great writer. He keeps having to write 'I must not bully' hundreds and hundreds of times.

What's the difference between School Bully and a hamburger?
Nothing – they are both Wimpy on the inside.

What's the difference between School Bully and the classroom window?
The window isn't cracked all the time.

What did the space monster
say to School Bully?
*'I'm keeping an
eye, eye, eye, eye, eye, eye, eye on you!'*

What's the difference between School Bully and an electric kettle?
Nothing – they both get everyone steamed up.

School Bully: 'I'm really going to go far.'
Class: 'Good – the further the better!'

Why did School Bully go to the Bureau de Change?
Because everyone kept telling him to get some cents.

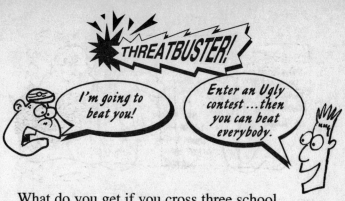

What do you get if you cross three school bullies with an earthquake?
A triple thick shake.

What's the difference between School Bully and a sore bottom?
Nothing – they're both no good bums.

School Bully: 'I'm a natural musician.'
Music Teacher: 'That's true – your tongue's sharp and your feet are flat.'

Why is School Bully like an oil well?
Because he's always boring.

Art Teacher: 'School Bully, you'd make a great model.'
School Bully: 'Because I'm so good looking?'
Art Teacher: 'No, because you're always posing.'

What do you get if you cross School Bully with a window?
A real pane.

Why does School Bully only eat curds?
Because he never gets his own whey.

What are shiny, noisy and try
to ruin everyone's Christmas?
Jingle Bullies.

Teacher: 'School Bully! Your homework is in
David Brown's handwriting!'
School Bully: 'I can't help it – I used his pen!'

Why is School Bully's cap full of cement?
Because he's a blockhead.

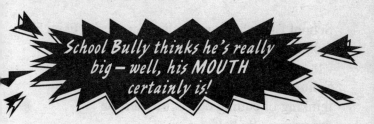

School Bully thinks he's really
big – well, his MOUTH
certainly is!

What are ugly, unfriendly and always saying
'Oranges and Lemons?'
The Bullys of St Clements.

School Bully went to a fancy-dress party as a
dragon. His costume was very realistic – he'd
only been there half an hour when St George
arrived and thumped him.

Why is School Bully always sitting on the ground?
Because nobody can stand him.

School Bully has a real talent for music. Even his feet hum.

School Bully: 'I've got so many muscles, I'm thinking of cutting down my exercise programme by half.'

David: 'Which half are you going to cut down – thinking about it or talking about it?'

What did the camel say to School Bully?
'You really give me the hump.'

Bob: 'You know what really popular
people eat for breakfast?'
School Bully: 'No.'
Bob: 'Didn't think you would.'

School Bully had lost his Pit Bull Terrier.
'Why don't you put an ad in the paper?' suggested
his mum.
'Don't be silly,' snapped School Bully. 'Fang
can't read!'

Why did School Bully's mum sew a lump of earth
into the back of his blazer?
Because his name was mud.

Why did the teacher stick a candle up School
Bully's nose?
Because he wanted to give him a light punishment.

First School Bully: 'I really hate Deirdre! After all the trouble I went to, that five pound note I nicked off her is fake!'
Second School Bully: 'Counterfeit?'
First School Bully: 'Of course I did – she had two, same as everyone!'

'Doctor, Doctor, not only am I a terrible bully but I can't stop telling lies!'
'I don't believe you.'

School Bully had his photo in all the papers during the school trip to the Highland Games. He didn't do anything special – he just went for a swim in Loch Ness.

First Dinosaur: 'I really hate bullies.'
Second Dinosaur: 'Well just eat the peas, then.'

Why was School Bully wrapped in silver paper?
Because he'd been foiled again.

School Bully dug a hole in the middle of the playground. We don't know the reason but the headmaster is looking into it.

Why does
School
Bully
always
wear a
metal
blazer?
*So that nobody
will be able to
pin anything on him.*

Teacher thinks School Bully should be an exchange student. She's hoping to exchange him for someone nice.

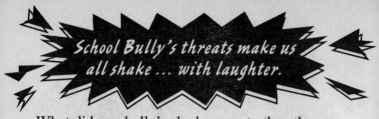

What did one bully's shadow say to the other bully's shadow?
'We must be daft to be following these two around.'

Teacher: 'Do you have any brothers or sisters?'
School Bully: 'No – I'm an only child.'
Teacher: 'Thank goodness for that!'

Mum: 'What's in this envelope – another complaint from your Science teacher?'
School Bully: 'No the bill for repairing the laboratory.'

First School Bully: 'It's not fair! All I did was give Sarah a little kick, and she gave me a really painful one back. What am I going to do now?'
Second School Bully: 'Limp.'

School Bully is a great actor. Every lunchtime he acts like a pig.

What's big and thick and chases skeletons around the playground?
The Skull Bully.

An old lady stopped School Bully in the street to ask directions.
'You look like a nice polite young man,' she said. 'Can you tell me the way to the opticians?'

What's the difference between School Bully and a caterpillar? *School Bully doesn't have a leg to stand on.*

Why doesn't School Bully try and frighten the school clock? *Because time will tell.*

School Bully was absent yesterday as he had to have urgent brain surgery. They were trying to put one in.

What do you call two School Bullies in a shoe shop? *A pair of sneakers.*

School Bully won the Biggest Bully Of The Year competition, but success hasn't changed him. He's still as rotten as he's always been.

School Bully: 'Are you trying to make a fool of me?'
Fiona: 'I don't *need* to try – you're making such a good job of it on your own!'

It was the school camping trip and the class was spending the night in a forest.
'It's your turn to go and fetch firewood,' Teacher said to School Bully.
'I'm n-not going anywhere,' he shivered, 'what if I come face to face with a werewolf?'
'Don't worry – I'm sure the werewolf will recover from the shock.'

I HEAR SCHOOL BULLY'S STARTED A PROTECTION RACKET!

THAT'S RIGHT – WE ALL BANDED TOGETHER FOR PROTECTION, AND NOW HE'S MAKING A RACKET

WAHHH!!

Why did School Bully cut the legs off his bed?
He wanted to lie low for a while.

Teacher: 'Who stole the headmaster's grandfather clock?'
School Bully: 'Not me – I'm only a small time crook.'

School Nurse: 'I'm a bit worried about that nasty-looking boil on School Bully's neck.'
Headmaster: 'You needn't be – that's his head.'

What do you get when School Bully forgets to bath?
A yobbo with B.O.

School Bully's parents asked the doctor to help them stop him fighting. The doctor put School Bully on a diet of carrots. 'After all,' he said, 'rabbits eat carrots and they are very timid creatures.'

Two weeks later School Bully's parents brought him back.

'Oh dear,' said the doctor. 'Is he still chasing people?'

'I'm afraid so,' said School Bully's dad. 'But it's not too bad – he usually trips over his ears before he can catch them.'

Why does School Bully never say an unkind word about anyone?
Because the only thing he talks about is himself.

What happened when School Bully sat on a tube of glue.
He came to a sticky end.

Why did School Bully have the glue in the first place?
He heard that school was breaking up.

Why is School Bully like a fly?
Because he's always in the soup.

'You can't always judge by appearances. School Bully has the face of a saint.'
'That's true – a Saint Bernard.'

School Bully could be friends with any kid he pleases. The trouble is he doesn't please any of them.

School Bully always wears rubber soles to the disco. He's hoping to get a job as a bouncer.

What's the difference between School Bully and a little lamb?
One grows up to be a sheep, and the other will always be a creep.

Little Jack Horner sat in the corner
Munching his lunchtime pie.
School Bully said 'Hey –
Give it here or you'll pay!'
And he did get it ... smack in the eye!

Why is School Bully like a taxi?
Because he drives everyone away.

What's big and grey and has no friends?
A bullyphant.

What do clever ants do if they get bullied?
Tell their par-ants.

WHY IS SCHOOL BULLY LIKE A BREAKFAST CEREAL?

BECAUSE HE SNAPS AT PEOPLE, HE'S CRACKED AND HE'S VERY UN POPULAR!

MARMALADE

'Teacher, Teacher, School Bully
stood on my watch.'
'Really? That's the first time I've
ever known him to be on time!'

Under what sign was School Bully born?
DANGER: GORILLA ENCLOSURE.

What's nasty, smelly and embarrassing and found
in School Bully's underpants?
School Bully.

TIPS FOR BULLYBUSTERS!

Bullybusting Body Language!

Bullies like to pick on 'easy' targets – especially people who look timid or weak. KIDSCAPE says that 'Body Language' is really important for keeping bullies at bay. Here's a simple experiment you can try to test this idea for yourself.

First make yourself as small and hunched up as possible, as if someone was about to hit you. Keep your head bent low as if you are ashamed. Walk around like this for a while. While you're walking say out loud, 'I am strong, I am brave, no one's going to push me around!' Bet you it doesn't sound very convincing!

Now try standing up as straight as you can. No matter what size you actually are, walk as if you're seven foot tall. Hold your head up high. Once again, try saying out loud, 'I am brave, I am strong, no one can bully me!' See the difference?

How you use your body really does affect the way you feel. If you carry yourself around like a victim, you are much more likely to FEEL like a victim ... and victims are just what bullies are looking for.

On the other hand, walking and behaving as if you are strong and confident actually makes you *feel* more confident. Don't worry if this takes a bit of practice at first – most of us have picked up lots of bad body language habits over the years. Keep practising and you'll soon find yourself behaving confidently without having to act at all. You can bet the bullies will see the difference too, and find someone else to pick on!

What did Tutankhamun do when he got bullied?
He asked his mummy to talk to the headmaster.

What did the TV set say to the bully?
'Just watch yourself.'

What's the difference between
School Bully and a science fiction writer?
Nothing – they've both got space between their ears.

Why did School Bully buy a big woolly jumper?
Because he knew it would have to be really thick to hang around him.

What's the difference between School Bully and a microphone?
They're both loud, but a microphone doesn't run away when you stand up to it.

What's the difference between School Bully and a bogie?
A bogie only gets up your nose sometimes.

What's the difference between
School Bully and Superman?
One's a big hero, and the other's a big zero.

Why did the bully chicken cross the road twice?
Because she was a double crosser.

Why does School Bully hate
alphabet soup?
*Because he's tired of always
having to eat his words.*

What's the difference between a School Bully
and Winnie the Pooh?
Nothing – they both have very little brain.

Why did School Bully buy a pair of roller skates?
So that at least he could push himself around.

What do you do if a bully sits in front of you at a
horror film?
Say, 'Gosh – I didn't know this movie was in 3D!'

What do you call School Bully with a banana on
his head?
A split personality.

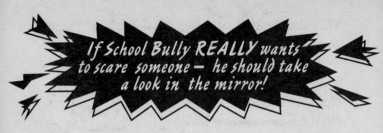

If School Bully REALLY wants to scare someone — he should take a look in the mirror!

Why did School Bully have a whoopee cushion on his head?
Because the joke was on him.

What does School Bully eat for dessert?
Cowardy Custard.

Why did the little octopus read *The Bullybusters Joke Book?*
She wanted to be well armed.

Why did the octopus need to be well armed?
The bullies at her school were real sharks.

Why did the monkeys hang around with School Bully?
Because they were out of their tree.

What did one part of School Bully's body say to the other part of School Bully's body?
'I feel like a bit of a plonker.'

School Bully jumped on Mark on the way home from school and was about to thump him. Suddenly a gust of wind blew School Bully's cap off.
'You stay here,' said Mark quickly. 'I'll go and get it back for you!'
'You think I'm stupid enough to let you escape like that?' said School Bully. 'You wait here and I'll go and get it myself!'

'Let me copy every word of your essay or else!' said School Bully.
'Here,' said David and dropped a heavy book on School Bully's toe.
'This is a *dictionary*!' howled School Bully.
'I know – but every word of my essay is in there, somewhere!'

'Dad,' said School Bully. 'Will you take me to the zoo on Saturday?'
'No,' said his father, 'if the zoo wants you they can come and get you!'

Why did School Bully swallow a magnet?
It was the only way to make himself more attractive.

What did the newborn baby say to the bully?
'*Grow up.*'

Jasmine: 'School Bully really should have been born in the Dark Ages.'

Jenny: 'Because of her prehistoric behaviour?'

Jasmine: 'No, because she looks terrible in the light!'

School Bully: 'Don't pay any attention to this *Bullybusters* book! If *I* had to tell my parents I was being bullied, I'd be ashamed to show my face!'

Billy: 'Don't worry – if I had a face like yours, I'd be ashamed to show it too!'

School Bully won first prize at the Halloween Fancy Dress but as usual he cheated. He wasn't wearing a mask.

Why was School Bully invited to the vintage car rally?

They needed a crank.

Careers Teacher: 'You should really think about being a doctor.'

School Bully: 'Why's that?'

Careers Teacher: 'Because your face has certainly cured my hiccups.'

What's the difference between School Bully and a jellyfish?

Nothing – they're both spineless.

WHY DON'T YOU WANT TO HANG AROUND WITH SCHOOL BULLY ANYMORE?

I'M TIRED OF HIM BEHAVING LIKE AN ANIMAL!

Mike: 'I can't seem to find School Bully in this class photograph.'

Spike: 'Look – there he is!'

Mike: 'No wonder I didn't recognise him – he's got his mouth shut!'

Karen: 'School Bully hasn't been well lately. Yesterday she was really miserable and grumpy.'

Kimberley: 'So she's back to her old self again.'

Headmaster: 'Why are the walls of the science lab covered with spots?'

Science Teacher : 'Because School Bully was messing around as usual. I caught him trying to invent a new kind of explosive.'

Headmaster: 'You mean these spots on the wall are bits of explosive?!'

Science Teacher: 'No – bits of School Bully.'

School Bully has a cold in his head.
In fact, it's the first time he's had
anything in his head for ages.

Why did nobody want to sit beside School Bully on the roller coaster?
Because he's always falling out with people.

WHY IS SCHOOL BULLY LIKE A WOOLY JUMPER?

THEY'RE BOTH A PAIR OF KNITS!

Why was School Bully underneath a big pile of furniture?
Because someone had turned the tables on him.

WHY DID SCHOOL BULLY TAKE UP KNITTING?

BECAUSE HE LIKES NEEDLING PEOPLE!

What did the monsters say when the ghost tried to bully them?
'We can see right through you.'

What's the difference between School Bully and a face cloth?
Nothing – they both shrink from washing.'

Ellen: 'School Bully's new nickname is *Amazon.'*
Helen: 'Why? Because she's brave and very strong?'
Ellen: 'No – because she's very wide at the mouth.'

Why is School Bully like a jigsaw?
Every time you shake him up he goes to pieces.

What's the difference between School Bully and dandruff?
Nothing – they both get in everyone's hair.

George: 'You must admit that School Bully is a person of rare intelligence.'
Georgina: 'That's right – he rarely displays any!'

WHAT DID SCHOOL BULLY SAY WHEN HE TRIED TO BULLY A SKATEBOARDER?

I DON'T KNOW WHAT'S COME OVER ME!

First School Bully: 'I'm nobody's fool.'
Second School Bully: 'Never mind – maybe you can get someone to adopt you.'

School Bully: 'I'm tired of you lot saying that I'm thick. My brain is in perfect condition!'
Bullybusters: 'It should be – it's hardly ever been used!'

I hear School Bully's descended from royalty – KING KONG!

How to Mess Up a Mob!

The only thing worse then facing a bully is facing a whole gang of bullies. Keeping eye contact, not looking scared, walking away – all the tips we've already mentioned are just as important when dealing with a gang. Below KIDSCAPE recommends some more tips which are especially good for coping with bully gangs.

Stay out of danger. Bullies don't hang around in gangs because they are strong – they do it because they are weak. Many of them wouldn't have the courage to bully someone who wasn't hopelessly outnumbered. That's why there's nothing to be ashamed of in getting away if you can.

Gangs tend to hang around the same places all the time, so it makes sense to avoid those places. This may involve avoiding certain parts of the street or playground at certain times or at least making sure you are not there on your own. Sometimes it may be safer to stick with a group even if they are not your friends. The wimp inside every bully makes them very scared of picking on anyone who isn't alone.

Become a gang buster. The most important thing a bullybuster needs to do is think very carefully about each gang member. Usually there are one or two ring leaders and lots of 'hangers-on'. Who do you think are the weakest members of the gang? Try and talk to these people on their own. They can often be a lot less brave away from their bully friends. Ask them how they would feel about being treated the way they treat you. Ask why they are joining in such a stupid activity. Many gang members only hang around a bully to try to keep on his good side – in other words they've been bullied into joining. Even if you can't get them to leave the gang you'll find that taking them aside like this makes it much harder for them to bully you. But try hard enough and you may well be able to persuade them to join you in asking for help together.

'Look, School Bully,' said Marie. 'There's no reason for us to fight. Let's just accept that we have opposite personalities.'

'What do you mean opposite personalities?'

'Well, I've got a personality – and you have the opposite.'

'Teacher says School Bully picks up things very fast.'

'Don't tell me he's started shoplifting, as well!'

School Bully: 'Hey you – what time is it?'

Marcia: 'Three o'clock.'

School Bully: 'Look, don't you try to be funny with me.'

Marcia: 'I'm not trying to be funny – what are you getting so annoyed about?'

School Bully: 'Why shouldn't I be annoyed – I've been asking people what time it is all day, and everyone's given me a different answer!'

WHY IS SCHOOL BULLY'S LEG STUCK IN THE POST BOX?

BECAUSE HE INSISTED ON STAMPING HIS FOOT!

School Bully: 'Whatever I say, goes!'
Bullybusters: 'Say your own name, then!'

Music Teacher: 'OK class – let's all get ready to sing.'
School Bully: 'No way – the only place *I* sing is in the bath.'
Music Teacher: 'Well, you can't have sung very often, then!'

School Bully: 'I hear you caught Angus mimicking me the other day...'
Teacher: 'Yes, but don't worry – I told him to stop acting the fool.'

WHY DOES SCHOOL BULLY HAVE TWO TEDDIES?

BECAUSE HE'S TOO MUCH FOR ONE OF US TO BEAR!

Teacher: 'So you want to be bouncer at the school disco.'

School Bully : 'Yes sir – I'll make sure to keep out anyone you don't want!'

Teacher: 'Good – you can start by staying home yourself, then!'

School Bully: 'Sir, Sir! The school football team threw my smelly socks out of the coach window!'

Teacher: 'That's not worth making a fuss about!'

School Bully: 'Yes it is – I was still wearing them at the time!'

School Bully: 'One more word out of you and I'll hit you!'

Mark: 'Coward!'

School Bully: 'Er ... Um ... t-that wasn't the word.'

As usual, School Bully was trying to steal the smaller kids' lunches. Barry arrived just as he was trying to snatch a little boy's bag of sweets.

'Huh!' said Barry. 'I used to waste time eating ordinary sweets too, but then I discovered these magic sweets. Every time I suck one I get more and more brainy!'

'Give me one right now!' said School Bully.

But Barry wasn't afraid of him. Like all bullies School Bully was a coward at heart but he really did want one of the magic sweets.

'At least let me *buy* one off you,' he pleaded.

'Fair enough,' said Barry. 'I'll let you have one for a pound – if you agree to leave the small kids alone.'

'I agree, I agree,' said School Bully, 'just let me have a magic sweet!' He handed over his pound, popped the sweet into his mouth and began to chew. 'Here!' said School Bully. 'This is just an ordinary sweet!'

'See?' said Barry. 'You're getting brainier already!'

'I didn't like School Bully much when I first met him. But when I got to know him a bit better, I found out I *really* couldn't stand him.'

I finally got School Bully to understand that words can be really hurtful. I whacked him with the *Bullybusters Joke Book*.

School Bully has a very even temper. Even when he's asleep, he's in a temper.

First School Bully: 'Somebody stood up to me the other day but I stayed cool!'
Second School Bully: 'I know – I saw you shivering!'

Teacher: 'You've been copying again. This essay on *My School Trip* is exactly the same as Peter's.'
School Bully: 'But I went on the same trip ...'

'Teacher, Teacher, School Bully's swallowed my text book about the Middle Ages, and now he's got the hiccups!'
'Don't worry – that's just history repeating itself!'

Why did School Bully
swallow a bottle of starch?
He was getting ready for a stiff exam.

School Bully's class went to a restaurant during the school trip to France.
Sandra was doing her best to practise her French but every time she spoke to the waiter, School Bully started laughing at her.
'Who cares about learning foreign languages anyway?' said School Bully
'You should,' said Sandra as she got up to leave.
'I told the waiter you're going to pay the bill for the whole class!'

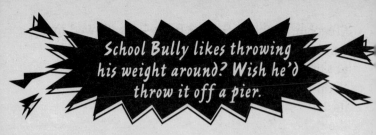

School Bully likes throwing his weight around? Wish he'd throw it off a pier.

Why was School Bully thrown out of Buckingham Palace?
They got sick of him trying to steal their rulers.

WHY IS SCHOOL BULLY HIDING IN A DUSTBIN?

BECAUSE THE OTHER PUPILS "REFUSE" TO PUT UP WITH HIM!

School Bully: 'Sir, the boy sitting beside me is preventing me doing my exam properly!'
Teacher: 'What's he doing?'
School Bully: 'He's covering up his answers.'

School Bully: 'When I finish school I'm going to have letters after my name.'
Class: 'Yes: T-h-i-c-k.'

School Bully is a really dirty football player.
Even when the kettle whistles
he shouts, 'It wasn't me ref!'

School Bully: 'When I catch you, I wouldn't
like to be in your shoes!'
Dave: 'I'd *hate* to be in your shoes – I know
what your socks smell like!'

School Bully: 'Dad, can I bunk off school and
come fishing with you?'
Dad: 'No – I've already got enough maggots.'

Why doesn't School Bully like *Coronation
Street* or *Eastenders?*
He tries to stay away from every kind of soap.

Gretchen: 'We learned about smoked salmon in school today.'
Gran: 'You mean you had cookery class?'
Gretchen: 'No – School Bully set the cafeteria on fire.'

The School Nurse gave the class an eye test today. School Bully was thrown out for trying to copy from the pupil beside him.

Claudette: 'School Bully, what are you doing?'
School Bully: 'Not that it's any of your business – but I'm writing a letter to myself.'
Claudette: 'That's what comes of having no friends, I suppose. But what does the letter say?'
School Bully: 'How should I know? I haven't received it yet!'

What do you say to a pack
of bully playing cards?
'I'll deal with you in a minute.'

Why do leprechauns never get bullied?
They've done an elf-defence course.

School Bully's really only misbehaved twice in
his life. The first time was all through Primary
School, and the next was all during Secondary.

School Bully: 'I really hate summer camp – I'm
homesick!'
Leader: 'Well why did you come here, then?'
School Bully: 'Because everyone at home is
sick of me.'

What did the baby say when School Bully
looked into her pram?
'Don't think you can push me around.'

Why did School Bully climb a tree?
It was the only way to get people to look up to him.

School Bully: 'What would you say if told you I was the Boss of this School!'
New Kid: 'I wouldn't say anything – it's hard to talk and laugh at the same time!'

PE Teacher: 'You've put your boxing gloves on the wrong hands.'
School Bully: 'But these are the only hands I've got!'

Have you heard the one about the bully terrapin?
He was turtle-y out of order.

Why did the crab become a bully?
Because he's always been a little shellfish.

What's big, ugly and snores?
A Bully-dozer

School Bully is in trouble for trying to borrow money. The pupil he was trying to borrow it from woke up before he was finished.

School Bully: 'It's your fault I've got a stomach ache! That pink chewing gum I stole from you was horrible!'
Jo: 'So that's what happened to my eraser!'

Why did School Bully have a sore finger?
Someone punched him in the nose.

73

School Bully: 'Don't let me catch you calling me mad dog again!'

Joseph: 'Why – what will you do?'

School Bully: 'I'll hit you across the head with my lead!'

Science Teacher: 'School Bully! Are you spitting into that beaker?'

School Bully: 'No but I'm getting closer every time!'

School Bully: 'What's your name, new kid?'

New Kid: 'Clarence Clark.'

School Bully: 'You're supposed to say Sir!'

New Kid: 'OK – Sir Clarence Clark.'

What do you call School Bully on a parachute?
Air pollution.

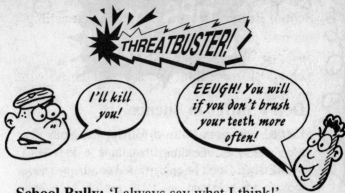

School Bully: 'I always say what I think!'
Class: 'It's surprising you're not a much quieter person, then.'

Jenny: 'I want to hide my lunch money where School Bully will never think of looking for it.'
John: 'Try putting it under a bar of soap.'

Teacher: 'Is it true that you've been bullying people again?'
School Bully: 'Er ... um ...'
Teacher: 'Having problems with the question?'
School Bully: 'No ... with the answer.'

School Bully: 'I don't know the meaning of the word fear!'
Naomi: 'Maybe you should buy a dictionary, then!'

Don't Suffer in Silence!

KIDSCAPE suggests that if bullying is making your life a misery, the most important thing to do is TELL SOMEONE. Don't be embarrassed or ashamed about looking for help and don't be put off by a bully saying that telling will make things worse for you. Remember that it's the bully who is the coward – otherwise they wouldn't be bullying in the first place. Bullies are only powerful when everyone lets them get away with it, so bullying is *everyone's* problem.

Tell a Friend. Sometimes telling a friend and getting their support can be enough to put a stop to bullying. Bullies usually pick on people who are alone. Even if the bully doesn't stop, friends can witness what is going on and help you tell your side of the story to parents and teachers.

Tell your Parents. Parents or guardians can be a big help in talking to your school about bullying problems, but remember that parents too, may need advice in knowing what to do. Some parents may even have been bullied themselves as children. Discuss the problem together and work out what you want the school to do before your parents contact your class or headteacher.

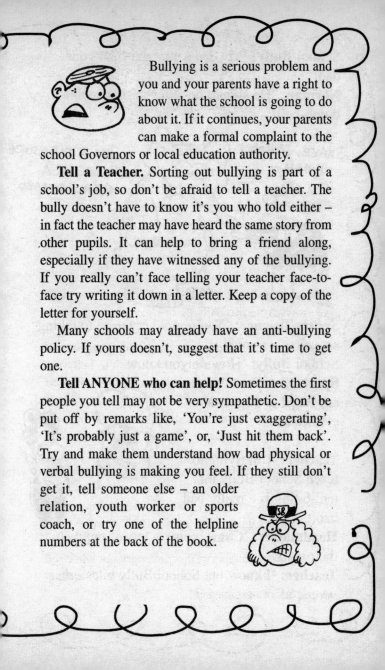

Bullying is a serious problem and you and your parents have a right to know what the school is going to do about it. If it continues, your parents can make a formal complaint to the school Governors or local education authority.

Tell a Teacher. Sorting out bullying is part of a school's job, so don't be afraid to tell a teacher. The bully doesn't have to know it's you who told either – in fact the teacher may have heard the same story from other pupils. It can help to bring a friend along, especially if they have witnessed any of the bullying. If you really can't face telling your teacher face-to-face try writing it down in a letter. Keep a copy of the letter for yourself.

Many schools may already have an anti-bullying policy. If yours doesn't, suggest that it's time to get one.

Tell ANYONE who can help! Sometimes the first people you tell may not be very sympathetic. Don't be put off by remarks like, 'You're just exaggerating', 'It's probably just a game', or, 'Just hit them back'. Try and make them understand how bad physical or verbal bullying is making you feel. If they still don't get it, tell someone else – an older relation, youth worker or sports coach, or try one of the helpline numbers at the back of the book.

School Bully: 'My dad's stronger than your dad!'

Norman: 'He should be, after raising such a dumb-bell!'

SHAKE, SCHOOL BULLY...

...IT'S A PLEASURE TO MEET A REAL DUMBO!

Sports Teacher: 'You're not very used to taking showers, are you?'

School Bully: 'How do you know?'

Sports Teacher: 'You're supposed to take your clothes off.'

Teacher: 'I'm trying to teach School Bully that nail-biting is a really bad habit.'

Headmaster: 'Come, come – lots of pupils bite their nails.'

Teacher: 'I know but School Bully bites *other people's*!'

How many of School Bully's gang does it take
to screw in a light bulb?
None – they never hang around anything bright.

WHAT BECAME
OF THE BULLY
CATERPILLAR?

HE TURNED INTO
A BITTER-FLY!

COMPLAIN! GROAN!

NO ONE LIKES ME!

School Bully was chasing Sharon round and
round in circles. How did Sharon escape?
School Bully had to stop and ask directions.

School Bully: 'This is a tough biology question:
"How long can someone live without a brain?"'
Tessa: 'Well, how old are you?'

Barbara Bullybuster: 'The only trouble with
this school is that there are too many bullies.'
School Bully: 'But I'm the only bully here.'
Bernard Bullybuster: 'Exactly!'

School Bully: 'You'll never be as good as me!'
Ahmed: 'I certainly hope not. I've set my sights a lot higher than that.'

Why does School Bully find it hard to make friends?
He can't find anyone who loves him as much as he does.

School Bully: 'If you tell on me, you'll be sorry.'
Bullybusters: 'Yeah – sorry we didn't sort you out weeks ago!'

Why did the Headmaster tell School Bully to stay in the basement?
Because he thought that deep down he might be a nice person.

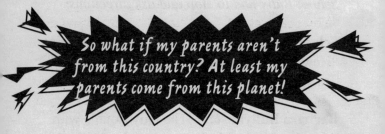

So what if my parents aren't from this country? At least my parents come from this planet!

Trini: 'Why does School Bully act so stupid all the time?'
Gini: 'Who says he's acting?'

Why did School Bully hit himself on the head on Friday?
He'd thought of a smart answer to a Bullybuster joke someone had used on Monday.

What does School Bully say when he wins?
Nobody knows – it's never happened.

Why does School Bully have to write his name on everything?
Because he's such a loser.

What's the difference between School Bully and marmalade?
Marmalade's only thick some of the time.

Why is School Bully like a remote control?
Because he turns everyone off.

'Hey new kid – I'm the School Bully!'
'I thought so – I knew there couldn't be a guard dog that ugly.'

School Bully: 'I'm the top guy around here!'
Bullybusters: 'Is that why your head's always spinning?'

School Bully: 'I'm a big name around here!'
Bullybusters: 'You mean there's a way of spelling 'idiot' with more then five letters?'

SOMETIMES SCHOOL BULLY CAN BE REALLY SWEET...

YEAH-TOFFEE NOSED AND ALWAYS IN STICKY SITUATIONS!

SWEETS

School Bully: 'I'm scared of nothing...'
Billy: '...except soap and water!'

School Bully is suffering from spots. The headmistress spotted him trying to throw his weight around.

Why do the kids in Legoland never get bullied?
Because they all stick together.

School Bully: 'I'm going to rearrange your face!'
Carol: 'No thanks – I don't think much of the job you've done on yours!'

What's the difference between School Bully and School Bully's finger?
School Bully's finger only gets up his own nose.

IS SCHOOL BULLY ENTERED FOR THE HIGH JUMP OR THE LONG JUMP?

IT DOESN'T MATTER – EITHER WAY HE'S BOUND TO LAND IN TROUBLE!

'School Bully's so thick, she put five pounds on my desk and then ran away.'
'What did she do that for?'
'Teacher told her to leave me a loan.'

School Bully had to leave school because of threats. If he hadn't threatened us, we wouldn't have told the teacher.

'School Bully's mum says he's got his father's looks.'
'I'm not surprised his father wanted to get rid of them.'

Teacher: 'Well done, School Bully – you haven't frightened a single small child today.'
School Bully: 'Yes Miss – but do I have to wear this bag over my head tomorrow as well?'

What did the dustbin say to School Bully?
'I'm not taking any more of your rubbish.'

School Bully: 'I'm going to be on the school sports team.'
Dad: 'How do you know?'
School Bully: 'Because Teacher told me if I don't stop bullying I'll be for the high jump!'

Why does School Bully hate ice rinks?
Because all bullies slip up sooner or later.

Teacher: 'How do you manage to annoy so many people in just one day?'
School Bully: 'I get up early.'

School Bully: 'So what if you've done a self-defence class – my feet are deadly weapons.'
Small Billy: 'Maybe you should wash them more often!'

Last night, I caught School Bully trying to nick my pet rabbit to help him with his maths homework. Someone had told him that rabbits multiply rapidly.

To Bully or NOT To Bully — THAT IS THE QUESTION...

PITY SCHOOL BULLY IS TOO THICK TO CHOOSE THE RIGHT ANSWER!

School Bully: 'I do what I like around here.'
Class: 'You mean you *like* being stupid?'

Careers Teacher: 'Have you ever thought of training to be a baker?'
School Bully: 'Why?'
Careers Teacher: 'Because you've got such a crumby attitude!'

School Bully : 'I got a terrible pain in my eye when I tried to drink the bottle of lemonade I stole from Mary.'
Doctor: 'Maybe you should have taken the straw out first?'

What's the difference between School Bully and school rice pudding?
The rice pudding really is tough.

What lives in the Arctic and has no friends?
The Abomina-bully Snowman.

THREATBUSTER!

You've been telling people I'm thick...

Sorry did you want to keep it a secret?

Why did School Bully put ice cubes in his aunt's bed?
He wanted to make antifreeze.

Why do astronauts never bully?
Because they can't throw their weight around.

Why did the skeleton make friends with School Bully?
Because No Body likes a bully.

School Bully: 'I made the whole school run yesterday!'
Linda: 'I saw them – they were all chasing you.'

Why did School Bully ask for extra lunch money?
Because people kept telling him to get stuffed.

What happened when School Bully was caught annoying people in the library?
They threw the book at him.

School Bully: 'I'm going in front of you in this queue!'
Patrick: 'Go ahead – it saves me having to look at your face!'

What's the difference between School Bully and a skeleton?
They're both boneheads but at least skeletons have some backbone.

WHY IS SCHOOL BULLY LIKE A NUT?

HE THINKS HE'S HARD BUT HE'S VERY EASY TO CRACK!

A bully who thought he was hard
Liked to push people round in the yard.
And then he pushed Sue
Who was good at Kung Fu
So we've sent him a get well soon card.

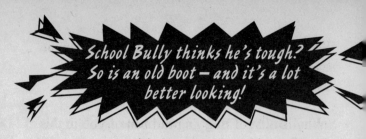

First School Bully: 'I hear you've been invited to Natalie's birthday party.'
Second School Bully: 'Yeah but she needn't expect any nice presents from me. I'm going to give her something cheap and nasty.'
First School Bully: 'Good for you. Would you like me to wrap you up once you've got inside the box?'

Why is School Bully always hot and bothered.
Because he doesn't have any fans.

Why is a garden like a School Bully's trousers?
Because they both have a weed in them.

Why did School Bully apply for a job at the shoemaker's.
He'd heard they were looking for heels.

School Bully: 'Have you ever seen a real live alien?'
Ravinder: 'No – you're my very first one!'

School Bully was caught stealing flowers from the Headmaster's garden. But he says that someone planted the evidence.

'Why is School Bully's head bandaged?'
'Teacher told him to wash behind his ears and the toilet seat fell on him!'

Why are Saturday and Sunday the only two days which never bully.
Because the other five are weakdays.

Why did the squirrel join School Bully's gang?
It wanted to be surrounded by nuts.

Billy: 'Want to know a good way to keep a wimp in suspense?'
School Bully: 'You bet I do!'
Billy: 'I'll tell you tomorrow.'

TIPS FOR BULLYBUSTERS!

Bust the bully blues!

Most bullies feel bad about themselves. That's why they set out to make YOU feel even worse. Next time you've got the bully blues, KIDSCAPE recommends these sure-fire ways to feel on top of the world again.

Make a list of all the good things about yourself. Don't be modest! Most of us are much too good at finding fault with ourselves even before bullies start making up new ones. EVERYONE has talents – learn to recognise yours.

Think Positive! We ALL have problems, but usually we make them even bigger than they are. We tell ourselves things like: 'I'm so ugly' and, 'I'm useless at Maths' which are guaranteed to make us feel worse.

It's just as easy to say the same things in a positive way: 'I may not be an oil painting but I've got nice eyes', or, 'I have to work harder at Maths but I'm very good at English'. Try it next time you catch yourself thinking negatively. We're positive it will make you feel better!

Join In! If you have a favourite hobby or sport like drawing, computer programming or swimming, think about joining a local club. Or maybe it's time you took up a new hobby? Your local

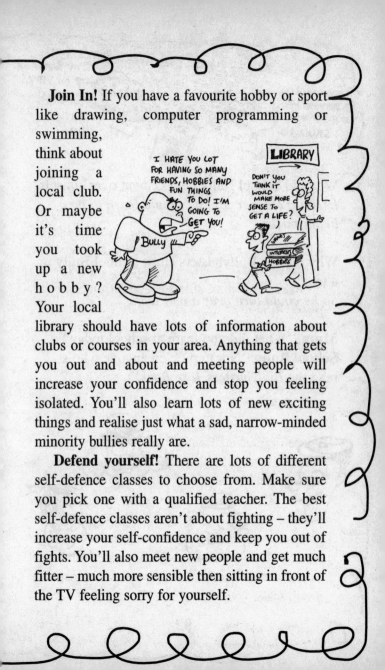

library should have lots of information about clubs or courses in your area. Anything that gets you out and about and meeting people will increase your confidence and stop you feeling isolated. You'll also learn lots of new exciting things and realise just what a sad, narrow-minded minority bullies really are.

Defend yourself! There are lots of different self-defence classes to choose from. Make sure you pick one with a qualified teacher. The best self-defence classes aren't about fighting – they'll increase your self-confidence and keep you out of fights. You'll also meet new people and get much fitter – much more sensible then sitting in front of the TV feeling sorry for yourself.

Why did School Bully pour cement over himself?
Because teacher said he should learn to be a better mixer.

Why did the Bullybusters chase School Bully up a tree?
So he could turn over a new leaf.

Mum: 'What did you learn at school today?'
School Bully: 'Not to pick on anyone who's read the *Bullybusters Joke Book*!'

BACK-UP FOR BULLYBUSTERS

If you are being bullied right now, we hope this book has cheered you up a bit. But being bullied is no laughing matter so overleaf is a list of places where you, your parents and teachers can get help and advice. You can also use this list and the other bullybuster tips if someone you know is being bullied. You can even get help if you think (whisper it!) *that you might be a bit of a bully yourself.* Whatever problems bullying is causing you, remember that being a bullybuster means you don't have to face them alone!

Organisations:

KIDSCAPE
KIDSCAPE provides information for parents, teachers and children. Free leaflets on preventing bullying can be obtained by sending a large SAE to KIDSCAPE, 2 Grosvenor Gardens, London SW1W 0DH

   KIDSCAPE also offers a BULLYING HELPLINE where *PARENTS* can get advice.
The Helpline runs *Mondays* to *Fridays* from 10 am–4 pm
Tel 020 7730 3300

The **Children's Legal Centre**
Tel 01206 873 820
This organisation can provide advice on children's rights.

CRE (Commission for Racial Equality)
If you are the victim of racial bullying, you can contact the CRE for advice. Contact them at their Head Office. **Tel 020 7828 7022**

You can also try your local **Citizen's Advice Bureau** (Check the telephone directory) or **Child Guidance Centre** (Check the phone book again under your local council).

Other Helplines:

Childline
Tel 0800 1111
Childline is the FREE national helpline for children
and young people in danger or distress. It's available
24 hours and all calls are confidential.

Anti-Bullying Campaign (ABC) Tel 020 7378 1446

Parentline
Tel 080 8800 2222
Your parents can phone this helpline
for advice from 9am–9pm on week
days, 9.30am–5pm on Saturdays
and 10am–3pm on Sundays.

Careline
Tel 020 8514 1177
Careline offers confidential counselling to parents
and children and the helpline is available Monday to
Friday from 10am–4pm and 7–10pm, with an
answerphone at other times.

If you need to talk to someone in confidence, you can
also phone your local branch of the **Samaritans**
(You'll find the number in your local telephone
book).

All information contained in this book was correct at the time of going to press.